Drubdra Khenpo Tsultrim Tenzin

How to Practise Dzogchen in Daily Life

Teachings in Triten Norbutse Monastery, Kathmandu,
on the occasion of Yongdzin Rinpoche's 95th birthday,
January 2020

Transcribed and edited by Carol Ermakova & Dmitry Ermakov

Public Series A

FOUNDATION FOR
THE PRESERVATION
OF YUNGDRUNG BÖN
གཡུང་དྲུང་བོན་ཉར་ཚགས་རིག་མཛོད།
WWW.YUNGDRUNGBON.CO.UK

Cover and title page photos by Carol Ermakova.
Footnotes by Dmitry Ermakov.

Published by
Foundation for the Preservation of Yungdrung Bön

FOUNDATION FOR
THE PRESERVATION
OF YUNGDRUNG BÖN
གཡུང་དྲུང་བོན་ཉར་ཚགས་རིག་མཛོད།
WWW.YUNGDRUNGBON.CO.UK

ISBN: 978-1-9169005-2-3
FPYB is a charitable non-profit organization. All proceeds from sales are reinvested into ongoing projects. Registered Charity (England and Wales) № 1173639

How to Practise Dzogchen in Daily Life

Contents

Preface

This public discourse on the practice of Dzogchen in daily life was given by Drubdra Khenpo Tsultrim Tenzin as part of a series of events – conference, rituals, initiations, teachings and cultural program – organised at Triten Norbutse Bönpo Monastery, Kathmandu, Nepal to celebrate Yongdzin Lopön Tenzin Namdak Rinpoche's 95th birthday in January 2020. Drubdra Khenpo spoke in Tibetan and then in English to the participants who travelled from all corners of the globe to attend the event. Many practitioners were impressed by Drubdra Khenpo's clear and inspiring delivery, noting similarities to Yongdzin Rinpoche's own teaching style, so, at the request of some of those present, Carol and I asked Drubdra Khenpo for permission to transcribe, edit and publish the English part of his discourse. He kindly agreed and has checked the final draft. It is our hope that both beginners and seasoned practitioners alike will find the explanations and instructions contained in this booklet of great benefit.

Proceeds from the sale of this book are donated to Triten Norbutse Bönpo Monastery, Kathmandu.

Thatsen Mustsug Marro!

ཐ་ཚན་མུ་ཙུག་སྨར་རོ།།

Dmitry Ermakov,
North Pennines, UK,
22nd August, 2021

About the Author

Drubdra Khenpo Tsultrim Tenzin[1] was born in Yetha,[2] Hor,[3] East Tibet, in 1968 to a Bönpo family of nomadic cattle herders. He entered Lungkar[4] Monastery at the age of nineteen, then Menri[5] Monastery in Central Tibet. In 1993 he joined Triten Norbutse[6] Monastery in Kathmandu, Nepal, where he studied Sutra, Tantra and Dzogchen with his root master Yongdzin Lopön Tenzin Namdak Rinpoche.[7] In 2001 he obtained his Geshe[8] degree (PhD) there.

In 2002, Yongdzin Rinpoche appointed Tsultrim Tenzin as Abbot of the Meditation School in Triten Norbutse, where he teaches Dzogchen and other subjects.

Alongside teaching, Khenpo Rinpoche practices Dzogchen meditation and Magyu *tsalung*, *thrulkhor* and *tummo*[9] for two hours every morning. He also travels widely to teach Bönpo Dzogchen, Tantra and *tsalung*.

---

[1] Tib. Mkhan po Tshul khrims bstan 'dzin / མཁན་པོ་ཚུལ་ཁྲིམས་ བསྟན་འཛིན་རིན་པོ་ཆེ།

[2] Tib. Ye tha / ཡེ་ཐ།

[3] Tib. Hor / ཧོར།

[4] Tib. Lung dkar / ལུང་དཀར།

[5] Tib. Sman ri / སྨན་རི།

[6] Tib. Khri brtan nor bu rtse / ཁྲི་བརྟན་ནོར་བུ་རྩེ།

[7] Tib. Yongs 'dzin Slob dpon Bstan 'dzin rnam dag Rin po che / ཡོངས་འཛིན་སློབ་དཔོན་བསྟན་འཛིན་རྣམ་དག་རིན་པོ་ཆེ།

[8] Tib. dge bshes / དགེ་བཤེས།

[9] Tib. rtsa rlung, 'phrul 'khor, gtum mo / རྩ་རླུང་། འཕྲུལ་འཁོར། གཏུམ་ མོ།

How to Practise Dzogchen in Daily Life

Good morning!

Today we will speak about how to practise Dzogchen[1] in our daily lives.

First of all, Guru Yoga[2] is of paramount importance when we practise Dzogchen meditation. Yesterday, Khenpo Tenpa explained how to do this, so today, I will begin by talking about *semtsol*,[3] searching for the mind.

Searching for the mind

Tibetan philosophers categorise many different 'minds' or consciousnesses. They talk about eight main ones and fifty-one minor ones. However, these relate to the function of the mind. Here, we are talking about the actual mind of each individual. One person has one mind. If you try to find this Dzogchen nature from outside, you will never find it; you must find it through looking back towards your own mind.

So, first of all, we need to search for the mind. We need to check thoroughly to discover where the mind is. This is very important. When we talk about searching for the mind, we need to think about where it is coming from, what the source is, what shape it is, what colour it is and so

---

[1] Tib. rdzogs chen / རྫོགས་ཆེན།

[2] Tib. bla ma'i rnal 'byor / བླ་མའི་རྣལ་འབྱོར།

[3] Tib. sems tshol / སེམས་འཚོལ།

on. We need to look where the mind arises from, and also where it disappears to. We need to ask ourselves where the mind abides before it disappears. Some think it resides in the brain, others – especially Tibetans – think it resides in the heart. It's important to understand where our mind abides.

It's also important to think about our emotions. Many people think that emotions guide the mind.

We should really try and understand where the mind is. Is it in the heart? The brain? Or in some other organ in our body? Humans are made up of many parts, and it's important to understand where the mind is, and whether it resides in any of these organs or parts.

Generally, we have so many thoughts while we are thinking – new ones, old ones, many thoughts. This is what we call 'the mind.' You are always thinking. Thinking about the past, or about the future. Right now, you are thinking. Always thinking. This is your mind. There are many, many different thoughts and emotions. So you have to check back again and again – where is this thought, this mind? What colour is? What shape is it? Where does it appear from? Where does it disappear to?

If you check in this way, then finally you won't be able to find anything that is the mind. The mind is insubstantial, immaterial. Yet still we are always thinking. If you look at this thought or mind, then finally it is just empty. You can't find any colour, any form, any entity, anything substantial, any characteristics. But you need to check this again and again. This is very important. Most people don't understand how to look at their mind. It's very important to keep checking this, and to ask ourselves where the mind is, what shape, colour etc it has. The more we look, the more we realise there is nothing to find. What is the benefit of continuously searching for the mind? Because in the end, we will finally really know for ourselves how to look for it and what it is like.

For example, when we have many thoughts, negative emotions may arise. For some people, anger may arise, or jealousy. But once we know how to look for our own mind, once we understand the Nature of our own mind, then it doesn't matter anymore if thoughts or emotions like this arise.

Nature of the Mind

Sometimes we get very angry. Very great anger can arise. Sometimes, not always. Well, I hope not always! So when anger arises, if you look at it, you can't see anything. If you look at the mind, there is nothing. We call it emptiness, but that means there is nothing. Nothing exists. There is nothing substantial, nothing concrete, no characteristics. It looks very, very empty. Just empty. So you look at your mind, you see nothing, yet at that moment, you are present. There is a very, very clear presence. You are not falling into unconsciousness. You are not falling into deep sleep. This presence is very, very clear. You don't see anything, yet it is very clear. This condition is called the Nature of the Mind.

Whenever a negative emotion arises, it is important to understand that the mind is empty.

First of all, of course, when we begin to practise Dzogchen, it is very important to understand the Nature of the Mind, how to look for it and how to recognise it. Sometimes it might be difficult for us to do this, but it is very important to keep our faith in the Natural State of the Mind and not lose heart.

In the *Zhang Zhung Nyengyu*[4] it says:

---

[4] Tib. Zhang zhung snyan rgyud / ཞང་ཞུང་སྙན་རྒྱུད། – The Dzogchen Cycle from the Land of Zhang Zhung is the most ancient of the four Dzogchen cycles of Yungdrung Bön. It has been transmitted uninterruptedly from Kuntu Zangpo (Tib. Kun tu bzang po / ཀུན་ཏུ་བཟང་པོ།) via the Lineage of Nine Buddhas (Tib. Bder gshegs dgongs brgyud dgu / བདེར་གཤེགས་དགོངས་བརྒྱུད་དགུ།), which includes Buddha Tönpa Shenrab Miwoche (Tib. Ston pa Gshen rab Mi bo che / སྟོན་པ་གཤེན་རབ་མི་བོ་ཆེ།), and then through the lineage of human masters right up to our time. The current lineage-holder of this tradition is Yongdzin Lopön Tenzin Namdak

"Suddenly a thought appears. If you look at it, it disappears. The thought, who is watching, watcher and watched, they all liberate by themselves into their nature. At that time, Dzogchen awareness appears to you" – *salewa*[5] means it is very, very clear for you – "That is direct wisdom."

རྟོགས་པ་ཆེན་པོ་ཞིང་ཞུང་སྣང་རྒྱུད་ལས་ཕྱི་ལྟ་བ་སྤྱི་གཅོད་ ཀྱི་མན་ངག་ལེའུ་བཅུ་གཉིས་པ་ལས།

།རྣམ་རྟོག་ཕྱལ་གྱིས་སྐྱེས་པ་དེ། །གཅེར་གྱིས་ལྟས་པས་ཁྱལ་གྱིས་གྲོལ། །གཏད་མེད་ཡེ་ཤེས་ས་ལེ་བ། །ཐོད་རྒྱལ་ཡེ་ཤེས་བྱ་བ་ཡིན།

This Dzogchen awareness or Dzogchen Nature[6] is sometimes called the Natural State, the Nature of Mind,[7] the nature of phenomena,[8] *thigle nyagchig*,[9] single essence – there are many, many different names but only one meaning, the single essence.

When you look at the mind, the thoughts liberate by themselves. They are not liberated by anything else or to anywhere else. They are liberated into their own nature.

Rinpoche at whose 95th anniversary celebration this discourse was given. This quote is taken from *Pith Instructions on the General Presentation of the Outer Views in Twelve Chapters* (Tib. Phyi lta ba spyi kyi man ngag le'u bcu gnyis pa / རྟོགས་པ་ཆེན་པོ་ཞིང་ཞུང་ སྣང་རྒྱུད་ལས་ཕྱི་ལྟ་བ་སྤྱི་གཅོད་ཀྱི་མན་ངག་ལེའུ་བཅུ་གཉིས་པ།
[5] Tib. sa le ba / ས་ལེ་བ།
[6] Tib. gnas lugs / གནས་ལུགས།
[7] Tib. sems nyid / སེམས་ཉིད།
[8] Tib. bon nyid / བོན་ཉིད།
[9] Tib. thig le nyag gcig / ཐིག་ལེ་ཉག་གཅིག

We say 'namtog',[10] which means concepts, conceptual thoughts. People often say that thoughts or conceptual thoughts are bad, but if you use them in the right way, they can bring Dzogchen awareness to you.

Thus, when we search for the mind properly, we gain an understanding of its emptiness, of the true Nature of the Mind, and once we have this understanding and experience, we just leave the mind as it is; we leave everything as it is.

When we understand the Nature of the Mind, it is important to maintain a stable awareness of it. Of course, sometimes we can't remain stable. But even if we can't keep this awareness stable for long, we shouldn't be worried about it. We shouldn't be discouraged. We should still try to practise every day. It's good to try and do this practice for some minutes every day. We don't need to worry, nor do we need some special time for this practice. Even if you have a job, you still have some free time. For example, if you take the train or bus to work, it's possible to meditate on the nature of your mind while you are travelling.

You need to remember it wherever you are – at work, while you are walking, eating, sleeping, going, coming etc. All the time, you need to remember. Again and again. If you do this, if you look at this state, then you will remain in it naturally, for a little while. For one minute, two minutes. Like that. In the toilet. In the bath. In your house. In the morning, during the day, in the evening, anytime. Even at midnight. If you wake up, you should remember this. If you practise this way, then spontaneously you become more and more familiar with this state. Whether you have extra time or not, it doesn't matter; if you always remember like this, then automatically you will become familiar with it. It is your best friend. It is very important to always remind ourselves in this way. And if we can remain in this state continuously for 20 or 30 minutes, gradually it becomes a habit. Once it becomes a habit, then we are stable.

---

[10] Tib. rnam rtog / རྣམ་རྟོག

So, we have looked at the importance of searching for the mind. Here, there are only four sentences, but they are very, very important:

"Suddenly a thought appears. If you look at it, it disappears. The thought, who is watching, watcher and watched, they all liberate by themselves into their nature. At that time, Dzogchen awareness appears to you, and that is direct wisdom."

In this case, *thögal yeshe*[11] means direct wisdom. This quotation is just four sentences, but they are very, very important. We believe these words first appeared from Kuntu Zangpo.[12] Also Shardza Rinpoche[13] – you know Shardza Rinpoche – said this is *yerig*,[14] primordial wisdom. There are many different words and terms in the Dzogchen teachings, but Shardza Rinpoche said that if you realise this primordial wisdom through these four sentences, they are the best gift from Drenpa Namkha.[15] This is the blood

---

[11] Tib. thod rgal ye shes / ཐོད་རྒལ་ཡེ་ཤེས།

[12] Tib. Kun tu bzang po / ཀུན་ཏུ་བཟང་པོ།

[13] Tib. Shar rdza Bkra shis rgyal mtshan / ཤར་རྫ་བཀྲ་ཤིས་རྒྱལ་མཚན། (1859-1935) – a great Bönpo master from Eastern Tibet who wrote many treatises on Dzogchen and participated in the non-sectarian movement (Tib. ris med). He established his own particular Dzogchen tradition and had many disciples, both Bönpo and Buddhist. At the end of his life, Shardza Rinpoche manifested rainbow body (Tib. 'ja' lus). For more information on his life and activities see: Gyaltsen, Shardza Tashi. Commentary by Lopon Tenzin Namdak, *Heart Drops of Dharmakaya: Dzogchen Practice of the Bön Tradition* (Ithaca: Snow Lion Publications, 1993), pp. 17-29.

[14] Tib. ye rig / ཡེ་རིག

[15] Tib. Dran pa nam mkha' / དྲན་པ་ནམ་མཁའ། – a great Bönpo master. There were three principal emanations of Drenpa Namkha. See Ermakov, Dmitry. *Bø and Bön: Ancient Shamanic Traditions of Siberia and Tibet in their Relation to the Teachings of a Central Asian Buddha*, (Kathmandu: Vajra Publications, 2008), pp. 144-149. Also, an on-line article can be found here: https://yungdrungbon.co.uk/2021/03/06/three-drenpa-namkhas-in-yungdrung-bon/

of mother and sister *dakinis*,[16] this is the secret path of the *rigdzins*,[17] the awareness-holders, or sometimes we say *pawo*[18] and *khandros*. *Pawo* and *rigdzin* mean the same thing; they are practitioners who realised the Dzogchen Nature and they are called awareness-holders. So this is the blood of the mother *dakinis*, the blood of the sister *dakinis* and the blood of the brothers, the *rigdzins*. OK?[19]

Union of emptiness and clarity

As for the Natural State, we say it is *tongnyi*,[20] or *shunyata*. *Tongnyi* is just a word, and the general meaning is 'emptiness,' but in fact there are many different qualities of emptiness. In Theravada it is said that all phenomena are devoid of self, that they are self-less,[21] and they say that this is the best view. Chittamatra[22] also talk about emptiness. Chittamatra and Dzogchen have many terms in common so they may sound very similar. Terms like *kunzhi*,[23] *rangrig*,[24] *tongnyi* and so forth. The words are the same, but the meaning is completely different. According to Chittamatra, *rangrig* means self-awareness, and for followers of Chittamatra, there are many different categories of mind, or consciousness. For example, 'eye consciousness' or the sense of sight. According to Chittamatra view, each of these consciousnesses is

---

[16] Tib. ma sring mkha' 'gro / མ་སྲིང་འགྲོ།

[17] Tib. rig 'dzin / རིག་འཛིན།

[18] Tib. dpa' bo / དཔའ་བོ། – 'spiritual hero.'

[19] Drubdra Khenpo explains: blood is vital for life, so here, the term 'blood' is used in the metaphorical sense to indicate something extremely important and precious. Similarly, 'mother and sister *dakinis*' represent the loving kindness generally associated with mothers and sisters, and of course, compassionate *khandro*.

[20] Tib. stong nyid / སྟོང་ཉིད།

[21] Tib. bdag med pa / བདག་མེད་པ།

[22] Tib. sems tsam pa / སེམས་ཙམ་པ།

[23] Tib. kun gzhi / ཀུན་གཞི། – the base of all.

[24] Tib. rang rig / རང་རིག – self-awareness.

clear to itself. Eye consciousness is clear to itself, mental consciousness is clear to itself, and that is why they use the term 'self-awareness' or *rangrig*. They talk about *alaya*[25] consciousness, emotional consciousness – they mention many different consciousnesses, and these are all aware of themselves. And they call this aspect self-awareness.

But in Dzogchen, and Bönpo Tantra teaching, the meaning is different. The name is the same; we also talk about *rangrig*, in spoken Tibetan, and that means self-awareness. According to the Dzogchen teaching, emptiness is itself clear; Dzogchen doesn't talk about the mental consciousness clarifying or being clear to itself. So this is completely different. Some people think that Dzogchen and Chittamatra are very, very similar, and Tibetan scholars often say this, too. But Yongdzin Rinpoche says they are completely different. Although all the schools give explanations about emptiness, they present very different qualities of emptiness. According to Dzogchen, you look at the mind, and this Natural State, the nature of your mind, appears to you. We use two words to talk about this state: emptiness and clarity.[26] But which is emptiness and which is clarity? Actually, this state is beyond all thoughts. Whatever thoughts you have – good thoughts, bad thoughts – it doesn't matter. No thoughts can understand this Nature; it understands itself. It is very clear to itself. This is very clear for you, too. If you look at your mind, this state appears to you. If you are thinking something, it disappears. So that is very clear for you.

Direct introduction

Nature is like that. Just like that. There are other introductions. For instance, *marthri*,[27] direct introduction. That is what this means. Without thinking anything particular, first you need to understand how to look at the mind. Once you understand

---

[25] I.e. *kunzhi*.

[26] Tib. gsal ba, stong pa / གསལ་བ། སྟོང་པ།

[27] Tib. dmar khrid / དམར་ཁྲིད།

how to look at the mind, that is what you do – you look at the mind, and after that, don't think anything. Just keep it naturally. Keep in that way, naturally. Don't think anything special, don't think with any intention, just try to keep in this natural state of your mind. Then, if you remain in this Nature more and more, for longer and longer periods of time, then you naturally become familiar with it.

That is the direct introduction.

Emptiness and clarity – these are different words but they have the same meaning.[28] It's important to understand this, otherwise different schools, different scholars and different lamas can say something quite different. Madhyamaka[29] or Chittamatra may use the same words, but the meaning is different; the quality of their emptiness is completely different. Don't make a mistake about this.

Emptiness and clarity in Sutra, Tantra and Dzogchen

We say *saltong*.[30] This is very important. *Sal* means clarity. *Tong* means emptiness and *zungjug*[31] means their unification. The unification of emptiness and clarity. The aspect of clarity is very, very important. If you lose it, and just emptiness remains, as in the Madhyamaka view, then it is just *shunyata*, no clarity. If there is no clarity in this emptiness, then that is not according to the Dzogchen view, or the Tantric view.

So remain like that, keep this in your life. Every day. Any time. You should remember this unification of emptiness and clarity.

Thus emptiness and clarity come to mean the same, one meaning, *thigle nyagchig*. *Thigle nyagchig*

---

[28] I.e. they are used together to refer to the Natural State, the Nature of Mind.

[29] Tib. dbu ma / དབུ་མ།

[30] Tib. gsal stong / གསལ་སྟོང་།

[31] Tib. zung 'jug / ཟུང་འཇུག

means single essence, single meaning. For example, 'fire' and 'hot' are different words but they have a common meaning. Or sometimes we say 'wet,' sometimes we say 'water,' but they share a common meaning. It's the same with emptiness and clarity; the two are inseparable. This is a very, very important point.

Emptiness, clarity and unification are qualities of the Natural State. 'Natural State' means your own nature. Absolute Buddha, primordial Buddha.[32] If you remain in Nature, you are in paradise! In nirvana![33] You are here in Kathmandu, but if you remain in the Natural State, then Kathmandu appears as paradise, for you. Only for you! Not for the general public. Do you like that? If you look for nirvana or paradise somewhere else, you will never find it. Just remain in Nature without thoughts.

Sometimes, thoughts can appear while you are remaining in the Natural State. If you reject them, that is wrong. That's the wrong way. Let thoughts appear. They appear naturally, but it's more important not to follow them, not to interfere. Just don't care. Leave whatever thought appears just as it is. This is the best way. If you do something with the thought, more and more thoughts and concepts appear. If you have more conceptual thoughts, then they snowball, always more and more. You have more concepts, they disturb you more, then you have more obstacles, more demons, more gods, more devas![34]

Remaining in Nature like this is not specific to Dzogchen alone. It is the base of both Tantra and Dzogchen. But not of Sutra. I told you, the view of Sutra is different; according to that view, there is just emptiness without clarity. That's the Sutra teaching; it doesn't explain about clarity. For them, clarity is just mind, it doesn't go beyond the mind. But in the teachings of Dzogchen and Tantra, however, it is explained that clarity is not our mind, it is a

---

[32] Tib. ye sangs rgyas / ཡེ་སངས་རྒྱས།
[33] Tib. 'das pa / འདས་པ།
[34] Tib. lha 'dre / ལྷ་འདྲེ།

quality of the Natural State – *salwa*. We call it *salwa*. We can say that the Natural State doesn't 'get dark,' you see. It is luminous, self-clear. And that aspect is called clarity. This clarity, emptiness and unification are common to both Tantra and Dzogchen.

In Tantra, they practise three contemplations.[35] They follow after thoughts. There are different types of thoughts – good thoughts, bad thoughts. This Tantra teaching focuses on good thoughts, while bad thoughts are negative emotions – anger, desire, jealously, pride, ignorance and so forth. Those are bad thoughts. So there are good and bad thoughts. Your Guru Yoga is a good thought. But still it's a thought nevertheless. Your *bodhichitta*[36] is a thought. Usually we talk about two types of *bodhichitta*: absolute *bodhichitta*[37] and relative *bodhicitta*.[38] We say that remaining in Nature is absolute *bodhichitta*. Relative *bodhichitta* is what you practise in the preliminary practices, you know. You are thinking about the welfare of sentient beings or something. These are thoughts. Good thoughts, very good thoughts. But they are still included in concepts, conceptual thoughts.

---

[35] Tib. ting 'dzin rnam gsum / ཏིང་འཛིན་རྣམ་གསུམ།: Contemplation of the Natural State, Contemplation of Compassion (The Four Immeasurables: Tib. tshad med bzhi / ཚད་མེད་བཞི། – Tib. snying rje tshad med / སྙིང་རྗེ་ཚད་མེད།, byams pa tshad med / བྱམས་པ་ཚད་མེད།, dga' ba tshad med / དགའ་བ་ཚད་མེད།, btang snyoms tshad med / བཏང་སྙོམས་ཚད་མེད།: Immeasurable Love, Immeasurable Compassion, Immeasurable Joy, Immeasurable Equanimity), Contemplation of the Cause – Tib. de bzhin nyid kyi ting nge 'dzin, kun tu snang ting nge 'dzin, sprul pa rgyu yi ting nge 'dzin / དེ་བཞིན་ཉིད་ཀྱི་ཏིང་ངེ་འཛིན། ཀུན་ཏུ་སྣང་ཏིང་ངེ་འཛིན། སྤྲུལ་པ་རྒྱུ་ཡི་ཏིང་ངེ་འཛིན།

[36] Tib. byang chub sems / བྱང་ཆུབ་སེམས།

[37] Tib. don dam sems bskyed / དོན་དམ་སེམས་བསྐྱེད།

[38] Tib. kun rdzob sems bskyed / ཀུན་རྫོབ་སེམས་བསྐྱེད།

As for the final goal, for Sutra, Tantra and Dzogchen the final goal is the Three Kayas;[39] we need to achieve the Three Kayas. According to Dzogchen, the Three Kayas exist spontaneously in your Nature, from beginningless time, endlessly. From beginningless up to endless. We use the example of a sesame seed or milk. If you want to eat butter, it exists spontaneously within the milk. If you churn milk, butter appears. If you don't churn the milk, the butter still exists there spontaneously, but you can't see it. It's the same with a sesame seed. The seed contains oil, and if you press it, the oil appears. But if you don't press it, you see nothing. Like that. There are Three Kayas in our Nature: Dharmakaya, Sambhogakaya, Nirmanakaya.[40] All three kayas exist there. But if you don't practise the Natural State, they can't appear. If, on the other hand, you practise with Nature more and more and finally become absolutely, ultimately familiar with it, then these Three Kayas appear spontaneously from your Nature. Whatever you need can appear. There is no other cause. This is very important.

The Sutra teachings say you need to practise the Ten Paramitas,[41] the Five Paths,[42] the Ten Bhumis[43] etc.

---

[39] Tib. sku gsum / སྐུ་གསུམ།

[40] Tib. bon sku, rdzogs sku, sprul sku / བོན་སྐུ། རྫོགས་སྐུ། སྤྲུལ་སྐུ།

[41] Tib. pha rol tu phyin pa bcu / ཕ་རོལ་ཏུ་ཕྱིན་པ་བཅུ། are: Tib. sbyin pa, tshul khrims, bzod pa, brtson 'grus, bsam gtan, stobs, snying rje, smon lam, thabs, shes rab / སྦྱིན་པ། ཚུལ་ཁྲིམས། བཟོད་པ། བརྩོན་འགྲུས། བསམ་གཏན། སྟོབས། སྙིང་རྗེ། སྨོན་ལམ། ཐབས། ཤེས་རབ།–generosity, moral discipline, patience, determination, contemplation, power or strength, compassion, prayer, method, and wisdom.

[42] Tib. lam lnga / ལམ་ལྔ། are: Tib. tshogs lam, 'byor lam, mthong lam, sgom lam, mi lob pa'i lam / ཚོགས་ལམ། སྦྱོར་ལམ། མཐོང་ལམ། སྒོམ་ལམ། མི་སློབ་པའི་ལམ། – Path of Accumulation; Path of Unity; Path of Vision; Path of Meditation; Path Beyond Learning.

[43] Tib. sa bcu / ས་བཅུ། are: Tib. rab tu dga' ba'i sa, dri med shel gyi sa, 'od gzer 'phro ba'i sa, phyag rgya bsgyur ba'i sa, bon nyid

These practitioners practise many different things, but, actually, everything exists spontaneously in your Nature. So, for example, if you practise the Natural State very well, then the paramita of generosity[44] already exists there. Moral Discipline[45] exists there. The Tantra teachings talk of *samaya*,[46] the Sutra teachings talk of moral discipline, but this quality exists already in your Natural State. The quality of generosity, of wisdom, of compassion – they all exist spontaneously in your Nature. This is only according to the Dzogchen way. Only Dzogchen understands these things. That is why it says you practise the Natural State alone. Sometimes you need to recite mantras or to visualise *yidams*,[47] deities. Sometimes you have a headache or a stomachache, and at that time, you need a pill, some medicine. In a similar way, sometimes you need to recite mantras and so on. But medicine is not your food, you know! Medicine is medicine, not food! So it's like that. This is like medicine, but it's not your food. For followers of the Sutra teachings, the Ten Paramitas, Five Paths and Ten Bhumis are like their food; they need them every day, all the time. Not like medicine. Followers of Tantra also practise many

---

sprin tshogs kyi sa, bde ldan rtogs pa'i sa, yid bzhin 'grub pa'i sa, ma chags dag pa'i sa, yi ge 'khor lo rdzogs pa'i sa, mi 'gyur g.yung drung sa / རབ་ཏུ་དགའ་བའི་ས། དྲི་མེད་ཤེལ་གྱི་ས། འོད་ཟེར་འཕྲོ་བའི་ས། ཕྱག་རྒྱ་བསྒྱུར་པའི་ས། སོན་ཉིད་སྤྲིན་ཆགས་ཀྱི་ས། བདེ་ལྡན་རྟོགས་པའི་ས། ཡིད་བཞིན་འགྲུབ་པའི་ས། མ་ཆགས་དག་པའི་ས། ཡི་གེ་འཁོར་ལོ་རྫོགས་པའི་ས། མི་འགྱུར་གཡུང་དྲུང་ས། – Bhumi of Excellent Joy, Bhumi of Immaculate Crystal, Bhumi of Radiant Light Rays, Bhumi of Transforming Mudra, Bhumi of the Billowing Clouds of the Nature of Existence, Bhumi of the Realisation of Bliss, Bhumi of the Fulfilment of all Wishes, Bhumi of pure Non-Attachment, Bhumi of the Wheel of Letters, Bhumi of the Immutable Swastika.

[44] Tib. sbyin pa / སྦྱིན་པ།
[45] Tib. tshul khrims / ཚུལ་ཁྲིམས།
[46] Tib. dam tshig / དམ་ཚིག
[47] Tib. yi dam / ཡི་དམ།

things. We mentioned the three contemplations, then there is what we call *chyerim*[48] and *dzogrim*.[49] *Chyerim* means you visualise the *yidams*. *Dzogrim* means you visualise the channels, winds, *thigles*,[50] *bhindus*, syllables. They need *detong yeshe*,[51] too, the wisdom of emptiness and bliss. There are many things. All this is created by the practitioners' thoughts. Good thoughts are OK, but it is more important to remain in Nature without any thoughts. Without any thoughts. Sometimes this is called *mitogpa*,[52] thought-less-ness.

Example, meaning and sign

Now I will try to explain about *pedontag sum*,[53] example, meaning and sign. This is very, very important for the Dzogchen system. I have already briefly described how to practise with Nature, and also the qualities of the Natural State: clarity, emptiness and unification. So now I will talk about *pedontag sum*:

> *Pe*, example, is *namkha*.[54] *Namkha* means space.
> *Don*, meaning, is *bönnyi*[55] – phenomena of nature, nature of reality.
> *Tag*, sign, is *semnyi* – the Nature of Mind. Or usually we say the Natural State, but actually it 'belongs' to the mind; it is the nature of our mind.

Example

So here, the example is space. Why do we use this example? Because we can see space directly, with our

---

[48] Tib. bskyed rim / བསྐྱེད་རིམ།
[49] Tib. rdzogs rim / རྫོགས་རིམ།
[50] Tib. thig le / ཐིག་ལེ།
[51] Tib. bde stong ye shes / བདེ་སྟོང་ཡེ་ཤེས།
[52] Tib. mi rtog pa / མི་རྟོག་པ།
[53] Tib. dpe don rtags gsum / དཔེ་དོན་རྟགས་གསུམ།
[54] Tib. nam mkha' / ནམ་མཁའ།
[55] Tib. bon nyid / བོན་ཉིད།

eyes. Outside, there is a big space, inside there's a small space – it depends on your house and so on. It looks as though there are many different spaces, depending on the shape of the room and so on, but actually, the quality of the space is the same. Space is space. According to Dzöphug,[56] Abhidharma, the universe is called a container, and all sentient beings, whatever and whoever is contained[57] within the universe, first of all appeared from space. Now everything abides in space, and, according to Abhidharma, finally, everything will be burned by the seven fires – *medün*[58] – that are nine times hotter than our normal fire. And there isn't only one, there are seven! There is a mighty wind, too, which is not like our wind. It may be nine times stronger. At that time, everything is blown away – the universe and all sentient beings within it. Nothing is left. There is also water; a huge flood appears and washes away the universe. So, first of all, everything appeared from space, now it all abides in space, and finally it will all disappear into space. It's not possible to go beyond space. Space encompasses everything, everyone, everywhere. So this is the example. Daytime, night-time, we can look into space, and see many different stars and planets in the sky – the sun, the moon, clouds, thunder, bolts of lightning. We can see many things, but whatever we see initially appeared from space. Now it abides in space, and finally it will disappear into space. For instance, it's cloudy now but in an hour or so all the clouds will disappear. These clouds will disappear into space. It's not possible for them to disappear somewhere beyond space. Everything is within space. This is the example.

---

[56] Tib. mdzod phug / མཛོད་ཕུག – cosmology.

[57] Tib. phyi snod, nang bcud / ཕྱི་སྣོད་ ནང་བཅུད – the universe is the external container and the sentient beings are the contents inside.

[58] Tib. me bdun / མེ་བདུན or Tib. dus mtha'i me / དུས་མཐའི་ མེ

Meaning

Don – the meaning: the Nature of phenomena. We say that whatever phenomena arise – the phenomena of nirvana or samsaric phenomena – there are these two,[59] but whatever arises first of all appears from Nature, from the Nature of reality, *bönyi*. It is very important to understand this. There are two aspects, two phrases: the Nature of phenomena and the Nature of Mind, but it is important to understand that they are of the same quality. We say *rangjung yeshe*,[60] self-originated awareness. It is the base of all phenomena – of both samsara and nirvana. That is why here we talk about the Nature of phenomena, because actually all phenomena share the same quality: they all stem from self-originated awareness. The self-originated wisdom which is the base of all phenomena is the same. I told you already, it has three qualities: emptiness, clarity and unification.

There are many universes, many sentient beings, many different things, so many phenomena. Some are connected to samsara, some are connected to nirvana. But everything first appears from Nature. Now, everything abides in Nature. Things don't abide forever, sometimes they disappear, so finally everything disappears into Nature. It's not possible to disappear beyond Nature. This is the meaning. Whatever we see – this table, house, all kinds of different things, the recorder here, the iPhones and so on – all these different things are called phenomena. First, they all appear from Nature. Now they abide in Nature, and finally they will disappear into Nature. Everything is encompassed or influenced by the Natural State. There is no outside or inside, that doesn't matter. Everything is encompassed by the Natural State. This is a very, very important point. The Natural State is empty, just empty,

---

[59] Tib. 'khor ba'i srid pa, 'khro ba'i snang tshul / འཁོར་བའི་སྲིད་པ། འཁོར་བ་སྣང་ཚུལ།
[60] Tib. rang 'byung ye shes / རང་འབྱུང་ཡེ་ཤེས། – also, self-originated wisdom.

but it has big *nyupa*[61] – energy, potential. Very big. Why? Because first of all everything appeared from it, you know.

I will tell you how. From the very beginning – we use the word 'beginning' but actually it is beginningless – five colours, five lights appear. White, red, blue, yellow and green. They appear spontaneously. Nobody created them. They are not influenced by anything. Without cause, without condition, they appear from Nature. At the same time as the lights appear, the mind appears spontaneously from Nature, too. There is no different cause or condition – just Nature. Then slowly, slowly, these different lights and rays transform into the five elements. Red light becomes fire; green light becomes wind; blue light becomes water; white light becomes space and yellow light becomes earth. So the five elements are already existing there. We also have these five elements within our body, the five internal elements:[62] flesh, blood, heat, breath, and mind. Each of these abides in one of the five organs: flesh abides primarily in the spleen; blood abides primarily in the kidneys; heat abides primarily in the liver; breath abides primarily in the lungs; mind (or consciousness) abides primarily in the heart. But whatever is there, it appears from the five elements. The five elements appear from the five lights, and the five lights appear from Nature. Spontaneously. This aspect is called the Nature of phenomena. Whatever exists appears from Nature.

It's the same now. We can see many different things, and it looks as though they were created by people, you know. But the very initial source is the Natural State. Then, after that, the five lights. This is a very essential key point which you must understand properly. In Dzogchen, if you are just familiar with the Natural State, everything that you have appears from the Natural State. Whether samsaric or nirvanic things appear depends on your understanding. If you don't understand this Nature, then samsaric things

---

[61] Tib. nus pa / ནུས་པ།

[62] Tib. nang gi 'byung ba lnga / ནང་གི་འབྱུང་བ་ལྔ།

appear from it. If you do understand the Natural State – properly, not just the words! – then from your Nature, nirvanic things appear. It depends on your understanding.

OK, it is like that. That is the meaning, the Nature of phenomena.

During practice, you simply remain in Nature. Don't analyse, don't check what emptiness is, what clarity is, what the Nature of Mind is, what the Nature of phenomena is, what the example is. There is no need to check. If you check, then that means you are already following after thoughts. You are already falling down from Nature, from your awareness. Your awareness has disappeared and this is just samsara. Samsaric things appear. If, however, you simply remain in Nature, there is no need to check anything. But you need to understand these things. You need to understand that everything is encompassed by Nature.

I will give you another example. If you look at the water of an ocean or a lake, you can see many different things shining there – reflections of stars, reflections of the moon, reflections of the sun, of trees, clouds, a rainbow and so on. There is also a reflection of your face there. Some reflections look nice, some look ugly. But if you touch them with your finger, they are all just water. There's nothing else. Some things look nice, but if you reach out and touch them, no, there is nothing. Some things look ugly, but in the same way, if you touch them, there is just water. There is nothing there. It's like this, you see. During the daytime, during the night-time you can see some things that look nice, some things that look ugly, or some things you want to enjoy, or something seems disgusting, something isn't good, or you see something else and think it's not bad, or so-so. There are many different things. But actually, whatever is there is just like a reflection in water. Here, we use water as an example or metaphor for the Natural State while the reflections are an example for phenomena. It's like that.

Sign

Here, the sign is the Nature of Mind, or *semnyi*. *Semnyi* means 'mind itself,' or the Nature of the Mind. You should understand that we use the word 'mind' in two ways. One is just to explain about the mind, but at other times, we are referring to the Nature of Mind. When we talk about our mind, we are talking about thinking something, so this is the same as thoughts. But now we're talking about the Nature of Mind, about how the mind abides. That is the Nature of the mind. It is called the sign. What do we mean by this? We can have many thoughts, many different thoughts. Since the teachings this morning, up to now, you have had a lot of thoughts, I have a lot of thoughts, too. Not only me, not only you, everybody has thoughts, different thoughts, but they all have self-originated wisdom as the base. All these thoughts – your thoughts, my thoughts, someone else's thoughts. So the Nature is the base of all minds. Therefore it is called the Nature of Mind.

Empty form

First of all, everything, everything outside there – the table, pillars, house, people, animals, cows, rabbits, cats – there are many different beings, many different things, but they are all empty form.[63] What does 'empty form' mean? I've already given you an example: in water, there can be many different reflections but if you touch them, oh, they're all water! There's no difference between all the forms. It's like this. Things look different, but they are all just empty form. If you look at this table now, for instance, you can't understand Nature. If you check how this table exists, using your mind and reason, finally you will realise it is empty. Yes, this is a table, but what makes it a table? Which bit? It has different parts – this side, that side, top, bottom, legs. Under the table, above the table, where is the table? If you check in this way, you will finally realise that these are all just parts of the table, not the table itself, so then finally you

---

[63] Tib. stong gzugs / སྟོང་གཟུགས།

can't find any table at all. This is like *shunyata*, which is explained by the Sutra teachings. If you check in this way, that's the result you will arrive at. You will never arrive at the Dzogchen Nature. So that is why you first have to look for the mind, at the mind.

The Sutra teachings also say many things about the mind, but if you search for the essence of things according to the Sutra teachings as I have just described, then you will never find the Natural State of the Dzogchen Nature. In Dzogchen, you just need to look at the mind. Then, as I told you earlier, at that moment the watcher and what is being watched are liberated by themselves into their own Nature. At that time, your presence[64] appears. Awareness appears. This is the sign. If you want to get the Dzogchen Nature, you must go this way. If you go another way, you will never get it. Never. If you want to become more and more familiar with this Nature, you must practise; it's not just enough to understand it intellectually, with your mind. You need to practise. Practice is very important. As you practise, you become more and more familiar with this Nature, and then slowly, slowly, all phenomena will appear to you as empty form. But at the beginning, it's very difficult to understand this 'emptiness' at first. 'Empty' means not solid. No substance. Like a rainbow in space – you can see, but you can't touch. That is what 'empty form' means.

If you are in a dark retreat,[65] many different empty forms appear to you; they are not influenced by your thoughts. They are not created by your thoughts. They just appear to you from your Nature. Not from outside. In the dark retreat, there aren't any different colours or shapes or things, so whatever you see is just empty forms that appear to you. This is the sign, *tag*. If you do this more and more, then more and more things, more visions appear. You must understand this. It is very important to remain in Nature. If you remain in Nature properly, we say this is called

---

[64] Tib. rig pa / རིག་པ།
[65] Tib. mun mtshams / མུན་མཚམས།

tregchö.[66] Then, in Nature, you can train with empty form with *thögal* visions. Empty forms are *thögal* vision. If you practise both *tregchö* and *thögal* and become familiar with them both, then the final goal is that your body disappears into light. Your mind disappears into Nature. Finally, you have nothing! [Laughter.] You like this? [Laughter.]

More on *Semnyi*

We have a lot of thoughts, you and me. Everybody has a lot of thoughts. So first of all, whatever thoughts you have – good thoughts, bad thoughts, neutral thoughts. 'Good thoughts' means thoughts connected to virtues. 'Bad thoughts' means thoughts connected with negativities. 'Neutral thoughts' means most thoughts, just general thinking. They are connected with neither virtues nor non-virtues. Whatever thoughts you have, every single thought, whether good or bad, first appears from your Nature. The thoughts come, they are moving, coming continuously, and they abide in your Nature. Finally, the thought doesn't stay forever; sometimes a thought appears, sometimes it disappears. It disappears into your Nature. Not far away. Like that. Everything appears from Nature. Now we are focussing on thoughts, on *sem,*[67] or mind, consciousness. All consciousnesses appear from Nature. This aspect is called *semnyi*, the Nature of Mind.

For example, now maybe you are gentle, without any particular emotion, without thinking anything in particular, you are just calm, sitting gently, then suddenly – maybe there is some reason, maybe there is no reason – you are getting angry. Anger arises. Check this anger. Where does it appear from? Where does it disappear to? If you check this, you will find there is no other cause, it just appears from your Nature. And finally, it disappears into your Nature. It appeared from your Nature, it disappeared into your Nature. During that time when anger moves and

---

[66] Tib. khregs chod / ཁྲེགས་ཆོད།
[67] Tib. sems / སེམས།

comes, it abides nowhere but your own Nature. Therefore, this aspect is called the Nature of Mind, *semnyi*. You need to practise this. Look at your mind. You don't see anything. Your presence is like sunshine in space; when you look into it, it is very empty. Space is empty, there is nothing there. Don't focus on anything. Don't look at the wall or at someone. Just look into empty space. It is very, very empty. Yet it is not getting dark. It is empty, but very, very clear. Like that. If you look at your mind, emptiness and clarity appear together to you, like space with sunshine. If you have an experience like this, this is Nature. Your Nature. Primordial Buddha. Maybe sometimes you become Buddha!

You need to be familiar with this. This is the main essence. Apart from this awareness, everything is like *maya*.[68] You know what *maya* is? Illusion. Everything is deluded, a delusion. Not trustable. If you become familiar with this, then whatever you want appears from your Nature. But not dollars! No silver! If something like gold appears from your Nature, it is just empty! You can't save or spend it! It's just empty form!

Everybody needs happiness. Nobody needs sufferings. As you become more and more familiar with this Nature, it will bring you more and more happiness. Your negative emotions, your very strong emotions, your worries, sufferings and miseries, whatever problems you have slowly, slowly disappear. Even if some very strong emotion appears to you, if you are familiar with Nature, it easily disappears. If you are not familiar with Nature, if you do not know it properly, it is difficult. That's why from now on, until you are familiar with Nature, you should practise. You should practise. That's why we say that this is a wish-fulfilling jewel, *yizhin norbu*.[69]

I have been explaining about the example, the meaning and the sign. If you understand this properly, then the key point is that there is no need to practise with

---

[68] Tib. sgyu ma / སྒྱུ་མ།
[69] Tib. yid zhin nor bu / ཡིད་བཞིན་ནོར་བུ།

different thoughts. Just keep continuously in Nature if you can. Everything is there in this Nature. The final goal is already there. I told you already. The body disappears into light and the mind, the conceptual mind, disappears into Nature. Then we say you have obtained Rainbow Body.[70] Sometimes we call this obtaining the Three Kayas. This is best.

Bardo

If you can't do in this way, then finally we are all going... we all have a visa for *bardo*![71] You have a universal passport

---

[70] Tib. 'ja' lus / འཇའ་ལུས། There are three main types of Rainbow Body. The highest level is Tib. 'ja' lus 'pho ba chen po / འཇའ་ལུས་ འཕོ་བ་ཆེན་པོ། – the Rainbow Body of the Great Transfer. At this level, a practitioner becomes a complete Buddha in his or her very body. Unnoticed by others, the physical body of such a practitioner is transformed into the essence of the five elements, the five pure lights (Tib. 'od lnga / འོད་ལྔ་); such a person does not manifest any signs of death. This kind of being can disappear and reappear on this mundane plane at any point in time or space in response to the needs of those seeking the path of realisation. The early Masters of the *Zhang Zhung Nyengyu*, as well as yogis from other lineages of Bönpo Dzogchen, such as Tsewang Rig-dzin (Tib. Tshe dbang Rig 'dzin / ཚེ་དབང་རིག་འཛིན།), all achieved this level of realisation. The second type of Rainbow Body is when the practitioner's body dissolves into the rainbow light of the essence of the five elements at the time of death without leaving any physical remains behind. This level of realisation is sometimes called the Light Body or Luminous Body (Tib. 'od sku, 'od lus / འོད་སྐུ། འོད་ལུས།). The third level is when the practitioner's body shrinks at the time of death until ultimately only hair and nails are left; these are considered to be external to the body as pain is not felt when they are cut. Sometimes practitioners do not attain full dissolution into the essence of the elements and their body shrinks to a greater or lesser extent. In such cases, although the practitioner has a high level of realisation, he or she has not quite completed *thögal* practice during their lifetime.

[71] Tib. bar do / བར་དོ། In this case, the intermediate state between lives.

there! You have a visa! Automatically! No need to fill in an application. OK. So, if you become more and more familiar with this Nature, then finally, if you can remain in this Nature when you die, then even if you don't take Rainbow Body, you will have a good helper in the *bardo*, a very good helper. If you are not familiar with this Nature, then in the *bardo*, even though you have a visa, you have no money! [Laughter.] You have no money... but the plane ticket is free. You can get into *bardo*, but you have no money. So you are homeless, you are like a beggar. But maybe nobody gives you anything. So this practice helps us very much in the *bardo* time.

Qualities of Nature

So, I have explained the sign and the meaning, and now I want to talk a little about the qualities of this Nature. These are very important. In Tibetan we say *kadag* and *hlundrub*.[72] Maybe we don't have much time so I'll explain briefly.

Kadag

Kadag means purity. This Nature is very pure from beginningless beginning, primordially pure. I will give you some examples. We say it is like pure water or pure crystal. Water itself is always clean, but if it is mixed with something, some silt or something, it can look very dirty. But if you leave it for a while without moving it, slowly, slowly it becomes pure. It doesn't matter whether you have mineral water or ordinary water; the nature of water is that it is always clean. But if there is some dirt inside the water, it looks impure even though the water itself is always pure. It is like that. In your mind, there are a lot of obscurations. Emotional obscurations, intellectual obscurations, many different thoughts, the five mental poisons – many things can appear, but they can't influence your Nature. All these seemingly negative states of mind appear from Nature, you know, but Nature is like water – it might look dirty, but in fact

---

[72] Tib. ka dag, lhun grub / ག་དག་ལྷུན་གྲུབ།

it is always pure. This purity is not created by anything; it is natural. We have many different thoughts – good thoughts, bad thoughts, any thoughts – but no thoughts can influence this Nature. It is always very pure.

We also give the example of a crystal. If you have a pure crystal and you put it into something dirty or into some mud, it will always be clear. If you put it in some mud, it might look as though it is dirty, but inside, it is always clean. The Natural State, your self-awareness, is like that. So that's why it is called *kadag*. Pure. Primordially pure. It is very clean.

Another example is that of a flower. A flower appears from something dirty, soil, and yet it looks very nice. We always use it to describe something very beautiful. For instance, we can say, 'Oh, she is very beautiful, like a flower.' This is a very common metaphor for beauty. And in the same way, as I told you, your thoughts appear from this Nature. I told you: look at your mind, and it appears. I told you it doesn't matter whether the thoughts are good or bad, or even if you are very angry; this anger is your mind, kind of. If you look at it from this angle, self-awareness appears directly. So it is always pure. From beginningless to endless. Nobody can do anything to mix it with anything dirty. That is *kadag*, purity.

Hlundrub

Hlundrub means energy. Big energy. This Nature has great energy, potential. Everything exists spontaneously in Nature. Good thoughts, bad thoughts, all phenomena, internal phenomena, external phenomena, whatever there is – everything can appear from this Nature, and that's why we call it *hlundrub*. *Hlundrub* means that something appears from Nature without effort, without creation. It just appears naturally. This is *hlundrub*.

So to sum up, this morning I taught you how to look for the mind, then I went through the qualities of the Natural

State, how to abide in the Natural State, and then of course in the second part I explained about the example, sign and meaning. And finally, I explained the two qualities of *kadag* and *hlundrub*.

Thank you.

Questions & Answers

Q: How do you link *hlundrub* and karma?

A: The relationship between *hlundrub* and karma. If you understand this Nature properly and are familiar with it, then good karma, bad karma, neutral karma – we call it *le*[73] in Tibetan – none of it is saved in your *alaya vijnana* consciousness.[74] But if you don't understand this Nature or if you aren't familiar with it and just keep following after thoughts, then there are good thoughts, bad thoughts and neutral thoughts, and this determines what kind of karma is saved in the *alaya vijnana* consciousness: good karma, bad karma and neutral karma. Neutral is neutral. As for good karma, it brings you to the higher realms in the future. Now, we are all in a higher realm, the human realm. We believe that the human realm appears from good karma. The lower realms – for example, we see animals every day, cows, for instance. We use them in many ways, we make many things from cows! Or from sheep, or goats. The animal realm is one of the lower realms, and they all appear from bad karma. Not just karma from this life, but from previous lives, too. If you save good or bad karma in this life, the result will appear in the next lives. But whatever karma there is, first of all it is all *hlundrub*; it appears spontaneously. It is very, very important to understand this. Some people say, 'oh this table is not *hlundrub*, it didn't appear spontaneously. A carpenter had to make it.' This

---

[73] Tib. las / ལས།

[74] Tib. kun gzhi rnam shes / ཀུན་གཞི་རྣམ་ཤེས། – 'basic storing consciousness.'

seems like a nice question, a nice argument, but in fact it is meaningless. For example, there are a lot of clouds in space, and rain comes down from there. Or snow comes down. But the source of this, the initial source, isn't a cloud; it appears from the ocean first of all! Some humidity appears from the ocean. If it appears over the land, we say it's fog, foggy. And then that becomes cloud. From the clouds, rain and snow come down. Many rivers flow down from snow-capped mountains, and the source, the initial source, isn't the snowy mountain; it comes from the ocean. In the same way, the table doesn't seem to be *hlundrub*, it doesn't seem to have appeared spontaneously from Nature, but if you consider a bit, you should understand the source of the table. The table first appeared from the five elements, and the five elements first appeared from the five lights. The five lights appeared from Nature. So the very initial source is Nature. That is what *hlundrub* means.

And karma is like that. You have all kinds of different karma, and it all appears from your mind, you know. Your mind. There is no other way. You are the creator. Your mind is the creator of your karma. Good karma is created by your good mind, good thoughts. Bad karma is created by your bad thoughts. Your mind appears from Nature. So the initial source is always Nature. This is called *hlundrub*. So whatever karma there is, is *hlundrub*. Understand? Aha, it's like that.

Q: If we are able to remain in the Natural State, at that time we are not creating karma, right?
A: Yes, if you understand Nature properly and are familiar with it, and remain in it, at that time, if you do something with your mind, body or speech, like working or something, then it is not possible for any karma to be saved in your mind. For example, Drenpa Namkha said: 'If you write in space with a red pen, there won't be a red line. If you write in space with a black pen, there won't be a black line.' It's like that. So, if you understand Nature and are familiar with it, then whatever you do with your body, mind or speech,

no matter what you do, it isn't possible for any karma to appear in your mind, neither good, nor bad, nor neutral.

From beginningless lives up until now, we couldn't understand this Nature, so in this *alaya* consciousness – we have eight consciousnesses but this *alaya vijnana* is special, we call it the consciousness of the base. It is the base of karmic traces.[75] We also say it is the base of Nature.[76] It is the base of all phenomena, not just of karma. Now the *alaya vijnana* consciousness is the base of your good, bad and neutral karma. If you understand Nature properly – it's not enough just to understand the words or the general meaning. If you follow the words, and think: this is clarity, this is emptiness, this is unification, this is *kadag* and this is *hlundrub* and just understand the general meaning, that isn't enough. You must also practise Nature. You also need to be familiar with this Nature. Then, slowly, slowly, the karma of your previous lives – good karmic traces, bad karmic traces, neutral and so forth, whatever – all slowly disappears, and new karma can't come to you. This is like the example given by Drenpa Namkha.

If there are no more questions, we will remain in Nature a little, then recite the dedication.

---

[75] Tib. bag chags / བག་ཆགས།
[76] In this case it is just called *kunzhi,* the Base of All (Tib. kun gzhi / ཀུན་གཞི།), and is not consciousness but the Natural State itself.

Suggested Reading

Gyaltsen, Shardza Tashi. Commentary by Lopon Tenzin Namdak, *Heart Drops of Dharmakaya: Dzogchen Practice of the Bön Tradition* (Ithaca: Snow Lion Publications, 1993).

Namdak, Yongdzin Lopön Tenzin. Trnscr. & ed. Ermakova, C. & Ermakov, D. *Masters of the Zhang Zhung Nyengyud: Pith Instructions from the Experiential Transmission of Bönpo Dzogchen*, (New Delhi: Heritage Publishers, 2010)
.

_____. *Essential Instructions of the Innermost Essence of Kuntu Zangpo*, (UK: FPYB, 2014).

_____. *Pith Instructions on Dzogchen*, (UK: FPYB, 2016).
_____. Transl., trnscr. & ed. Nagru Geshe Gelek Jinpa, Ermakova, C. & Ermakov, D. *The Heart Essence of the Khandro, Experiential Instructions on Bönpo Dzogchen: Thirty Signs and Meanings from Women Lineage-Holders*, (New Delhi: Heritage Publishers, 2012).

_____. Trnscr. & ed. John Myrdhin Reynolds, *Bonpo Dzogchen Teachings*, (Kathmandu: Vajra Publications, 2006).

Nyima, Menri Tridzin Lungtog Tenpai. *Approaching Dzogchen according to the Athri Cycle*, (UK: FPYB, 2016).

Notes